Explore Earth

Jackie Golusky

Lerner Publications ◆ Minneapolis

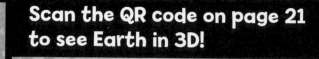

PAGE PLUS

Scan the QR code on page 21 to see Earth in 3D!

Lerner Publications Company
An imprint of Lerner Publishing Group, Inc.
241 First Avenue North
Minneapolis, MN 55401 USA

For reading levels and more information, look up this title at www.lernerbooks.com.

Main body text set in Billy Infant regular.
Typeface provided by SparkType.

Library of Congress Cataloging-in-Publication Data

Names: Golusky, Jackie, 1996- author.
Title: Explore Earth / Jackie Golusky.
Other titles: Lightning bolt books. Planet explorer.
Description: Minneapolis, MN : Lerner Publications, [2021] | Series: Lightning bolt books - Planet explorer | Includes bibliographical references and index. | Audience: Ages 6-9 | Audience: Grades 2-3 | Summary: "Readers learn what makes Earth so unique among the planets in our solar system. This title covers Earth's formation, the unique presence of life, and climate change"— Provided by publisher.
Identifiers: LCCN 2020009472 (print) | LCCN 2020009473 (ebook) | ISBN 9781728404080 (library binding) | ISBN 9781728418445 (ebook)
Subjects: LCSH: Earth (Planet)—Juvenile literature.
Classification: LCC QB631.4 .G657 2021 (print) | LCC QB631.4 (ebook) | DDC 550—dc23

LC record available at https://lccn.loc.gov/2020009472
LC ebook record available at https://lccn.loc.gov/2020009473

Manufactured in the United States of America
1-48466-48980-5/28/2020

Table of Contents

All about Earth

Red rocks surround you. You aren't on Mars. You're on Earth!

Mercury Venus Earth Mars Jupiter Saturn Uranus Neptune

This diagram shows the order of the planets in the solar system.

Earth is a planet in the solar system. It is the third planet from our star, the sun. It is about 93 million miles (150 million km) from the sun.

Earth is 7,918 miles (12,743 km) across, while the sun is about 864,400 miles (1.39 million km) across. More than one million Earths could fit inside the sun.

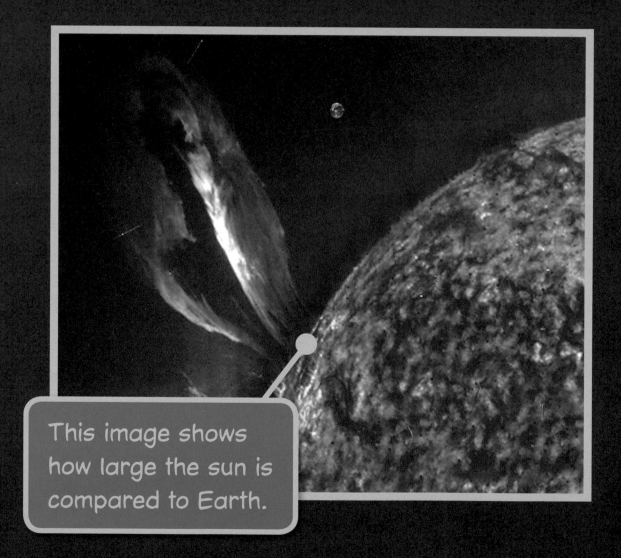

This image shows how large the sun is compared to Earth.

Earth is a rocky planet. It is made up mostly of metals and rocks. Earth is the largest rocky planet and the fifth-largest planet in our solar system.

These are the rocky planets in the solar system. *From top to bottom*, they are Mars, Earth, Venus, and Mercury.

Earth's Moon

Earth has one moon. The moon goes around Earth in an oval-shaped path called an orbit. It takes the moon about twenty-seven days to orbit Earth.

Many scientists think the moon was created when a large object crashed into Earth billions of years ago.

Rocky objects crashed into the moon and left behind huge craters. One crater is more than 52 miles (84 km) wide.

On February 15, 2020, scientists discovered a small rock orbiting Earth. They called the rock a mini-moon. The mini-moon is about the size of a washing machine.

Scientists believe Earth has had many mini-moons throughout its history.

Earth's gravity pulled the mini-moon into orbit in 2017. But the mini-moon orbited for only a few years before Earth's gravity flung it away in 2020.

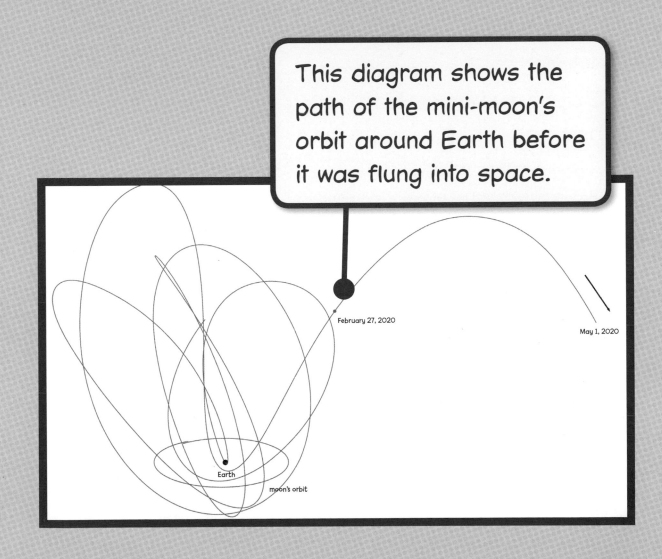

This diagram shows the path of the mini-moon's orbit around Earth before it was flung into space.

Living on Earth

Earth has a lot of water and a breathable atmosphere. It is just the right distance from the sun to help it support life. If it were closer, it would be too hot. If it were farther away, it would be too cold.

Earth is tilted on an axis. This tilt causes seasons. When Earth's side is tilted toward the sun, it's summer on that side. When a side is tilted away, it's winter on that side.

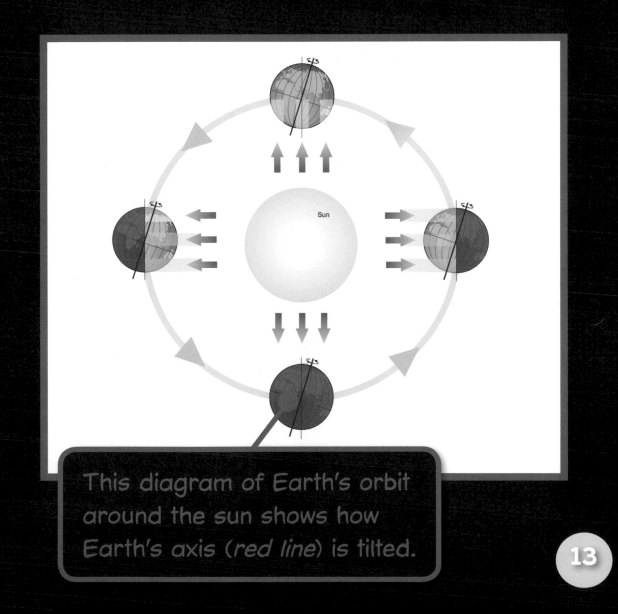

This diagram of Earth's orbit around the sun shows how Earth's axis (*red line*) is tilted.

Photos from space of places near Earth's equator show bright blue water and green forests.

The equator is an invisible line around the middle of Earth. Earth is warmer along its equator. The equator stays hot because it doesn't tilt far away from the sun.

Climate change is changing Earth. The atmosphere has gases that can trap heat. This heat causes glaciers to melt and sea levels to rise. It can also cause more severe weather.

A glacier is a huge chunk of ice that flows very slowly across land.

Checking Out Earth

NASA's Artemis program wants to send astronauts to the moon by 2024. The astronauts will explore more of the moon. They hope to find water on it.

A submarine holds out bait to attract a deep-sea snailfish.

Oceans cover most of Earth, but scientists have explored only 5 percent of them. In 2014, scientists discovered snailfish living 26,722 feet (8,145 m) underwater. Before, people didn't think anything could live that deep in the ocean.

The Sentinel-6A spacecraft sits in a clean room before launch. Spacecraft must be kept clean because dirty equipment can ruin a launch.

Scientists study the ocean from space during the Sentinel-6/Jason-CS mission. The mission will track sea levels until 2030. Scientists want to see how much the sea levels rise due to climate change.

Scientists are always discovering new things about Earth and its moon.

Aboard the International Space Station, astronauts can see Earth like never before.

Planet Facts

- A year on Earth is 365.25 days, so after four years we have one extra day. This is why we have leap day every four years.

- The moon is 238,855 miles (384,400 km) away from Earth, meaning thirty Earths could fit between Earth and the moon.

- Scientists often measure distances in outer space in astronomical units (AU). One AU is the distance from the sun to Earth. So Earth is one AU from the sun.

Space Story

Earth is the only planet in our solar system not named after a Greek or Roman god or goddess. It's named after the German word for "ground."

Scan the QR code to the right to see Earth in 3D!

Glossary

atmosphere: the air that surrounds Earth

axis: an invisible line that Earth turns around

climate change: a change in weather conditions over time due to gases that trap heat

crater: a large round hole in the ground

gas: material that is like air and has no fixed shape

glacier: a huge piece of ice

gravity: a force that pulls things together

mini-moon: a small rock that orbits a planet for a short period of time

solar system: a star and the planets that move around it

weather: the temperature and other outside conditions

Learn More

Brundle, Joanna. *The Scale of the Solar System*. New York: Crabtree, 2020.

Golusky, Jackie. *Explore Mars*. Minneapolis: Lerner Publications, 2021.

NASA: All about Earth
https://spaceplace.nasa.gov/all-about-earth/en/

NASA: What Is Happening in the Ocean?
https://climatekids.nasa.gov/ocean/

National Geographic Kids: Mission to Earth
https://kids.nationalgeographic.com/explore/space/mission-to-earth/

Rector, Rebecca Kraft. *The Moon*. New York: Enslow, 2019.

Index

Photo Acknowledgments

Image credits: Edwin Verin/Shutterstock.com, p. 4; WP/Wikimedia Commons (CC BY-SA 3.0), p. 5; NASA/GSFC/SOHO/ESA (CC BY 2.0), p. 6; NASA/JHUAPL (Mercury); NASA (Venus); Nasa/Apollo 17 crew (Earth); ESA/MPS/UPD/LAM/IAA/RSSD/INTA/UPM/DASP/IDA/ (Mars); Wikimedia Commons, p. 7; NASA/JPL/USGS, p. 8; NASA/JPL-Caltech/T. Pyle (SSC), p. 9; NASA/JPL-Caltech, p. 10; NASA/JPL/Javier Roa Vicens, p. 11; NASA, pp. 12, 14, 16, 19; Soleil Nordic/Shutterstock.com, p. 13; Martin St-Amant/Wikimedia Commons (CC BY-SA 3.0), p. 15; Dr Alan Jamieson and Dr Thomas Linley, Newcastle University. RV Sonne voyage SO261, HADES-ERC, p. 17; NASA/IABG, p. 18.

Cover: NASA/NOAA/GSFC/Suomi NPP/VIIRS/Norman Kuring.